DO YOU REALLY WANT TO MEET A POLAR BEAR?

WRITTEN BY MARCIE ABOFF   ILLUSTRATED BY DANIELE FABBRI

Amicus Illustrated and Amicus Ink
are published by Amicus
P.O. Box 227, Mankato, MN 56002
www.amicuspublishing.us

Copyright © 2015 Amicus. International copyright reserved in all countries. No part of this book may be reproduced in any form without written permission from the publisher.

Paperback ISBN: 978-1-62243-230-1

Library of Congress Cataloging-in-Publication Data
Aboff, Marcie, author.
Do you really want to meet a polar bear? / Marcie Aboff; illustrated by Daniele Fabbri.
   pages cm. — (Do you really want to meet?)
Summary: "A boy is bored with research for his school report so he decides to visit the Arctic and learn about polar bears firsthand"— Provided by publisher.
  Audience: Grade K to 3.
  Includes bibliographical references and index.
  ISBN 978-1-60753-455-6 (library binding) —
  ISBN 978-1-60753-670-3 (ebook)
  1. Polar bear—Juvenile literature. 2. North Pole—Juvenile literature. I. Fabbri, Daniele, 1978- ill. II. Title.
  QL737.C27A26 2015
  599.786—dc23   2013034684

Editor: Rebecca Glaser
Designer: Kathleen Petelinsek

ABOUT THE AUTHOR

Marcie Aboff is the author more than 50 books and magazine stories, including works featuring dogs, cats, owls, and brown bears. This is her first book about polar bears. She lives in New Jersey with her family and Pomeranian dog. Visit Marcie on her website, www.marcieaboff.com.

ABOUT THE ILLUSTRATOR

Daniele Fabbri was born in Ravenna, Italy, in 1978. He graduated from Istituto Europeo di Design in Milan, Italy, and started his career as a cartoon animator, storyboarder, and background designer for animated series. He has worked as a freelance illustrator since 2003, collaborating with international publishers and advertising agencies.

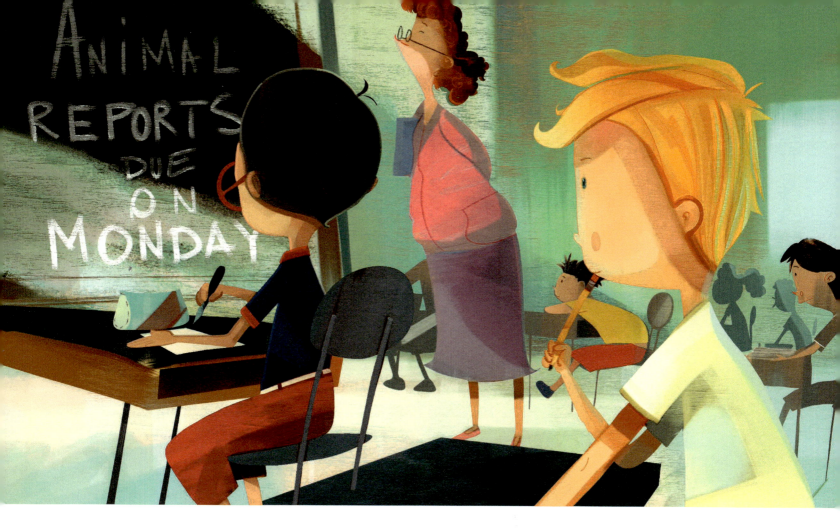

Your report on polar bears is due next week. You could do some research. But wouldn't it be fun to go to the North Pole and meet a *real* polar bear?

Pack lots of heavy sweaters and snow pants. You could get frostbite if your skin isn't covered. And bring three pairs of gloves. You might need to wear all three at the same time!

After flying many hours, your airplane finally reaches the snow-covered Arctic. It's bitter cold.

Ready to explore, you trudge through the snow. What are these big paw prints? The back paws are twice the size of the front paws.

You spot a huge polar bear ahead! Some male polar bears weigh as much as 1,700 pounds (771 kg). You're not going to ride one of those big boys any time soon!

Surprise! Polar bears aren't white. Their fur strands are really clear. The fur reflects the snow and sunlight, making them look white.

You move a little closer to the bear.
He's sitting by a hole in the ice.

Suddenly, a seal raises his head though the breathing hole. The polar bear grabs the seal. The bear's sharp claws and jagged teeth attack his meal.

Back at camp, you jump on your snowmobile. You spot a mother and her two cubs on a snow bank. It's early spring and they're rambling out of their den.

Don't even think about petting the cute, cuddly-looking cubs. Mama might get angry. She'll fight to protect her cubs.

You zoom away. The cold wind whips across your face. Polar bears cover a large range, and adults are usually solitary, staying by themselves.

Finally you spot another polar bear on an ice floe. He's diving for food. Don't jump in after him. You don't have a thick layer of blubber to protect you from icy, sub-zero waters like he does.

Polar bears are excellent swimmers. They can swim up to 100 miles (160 km) at a time.

You move in close.

The bear climbs out of the water. He's coming in your direction! His rough paw pads help him quickly move across the ice and snow. He's taller than you. And your heart is pounding!

Whew—just made it! Polar bears don't usually attack people, but you'd rather not take any chances. You're freezing, too. Time to leave.

It's great to be home. Your spring jacket feels a lot better than five layers of clothes. But it was a fun trip—and you have plenty of firsthand research to write your report.

WHERE DO POLAR BEARS LIVE?

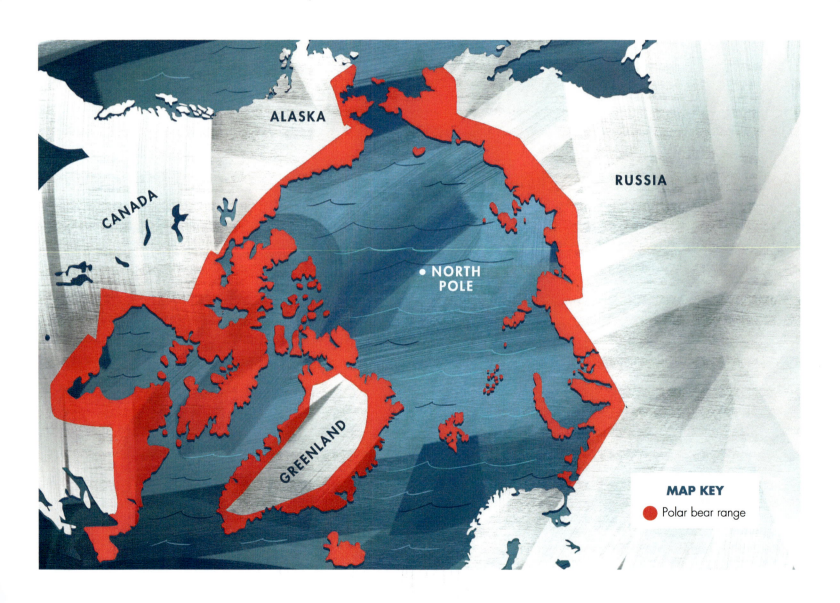

GLOSSARY

Arctic The North Pole and regions near it.

blubber The fat of large ocean animals; blubber keeps them warm.

breathing hole A hole in ice made by seals so they can come up to breathe.

ice floe A large floating mass of sea ice.

range The place where a certain kind of animal lives.

solitary Being alone without companions.

trudge A slow, tiresome walk.

READ MORE

Bodden, Valerie. **Polar Bears**. Mankato, Minn.: Creative Education, 2010.

Markle, Sandra. **Waiting for Ice**. Watertown, Mass.: Charlesbridge, 2012.

Marsh, Laura F. **Polar Bears**. Washington, D.C.: National Geographic, 2013.

Marsico, Katie. **Polar Bear**. Chicago: Heinemann-Raintree, 2012.

Turnbull, Stephanie. **Polar Bear**. Mankato, Minn.: Smart Apple Media, 2013.

WEBSITES

Discovery Kids : Tell Me—Polar Bears
http://kids.discovery.com/tell-me/animals/mammals/polar-bears
Read information and see pictures of polar bears.

Polar Bear Facts and Pictures—National Geographic Kids
http://kids.nationalgeographic.com/kids/animals/creaturefeature/polar-bear/
See a polar bear video and hear what polar bears sound like.

Polar Bears for Kids | Polar Bears International
http://www.polarbearsinternational.org/for-students/polar-bears-for-kids
This site has information about polar bears with pictures, and includes a research section for kids doing reports.

The San Diego Zoo's Polar Cam: Meet the Polar Bears
http://www.sandiegozoo.org/polarcam/meet.html
Learn about the three polar bears that live at the San Diego Zoo and watch their activity live with the polar cam.

Every effort has been made to ensure that these websites are appropriate for children. However, because of the nature of the Internet, it is impossible to guarantee that these sites will remain active indefinitely or that their contents will not be altered.